Manage Your Money

A 12 Month Budget Planner to Transform Your Finances

MANAGE YOUR MONEY

Written by Tyler N. Media

belongs to

____

TABLE OF CONTENTS

Introduction 7

Step 1: Determine My Money Mindset 9

Step 2: Set Financial Goals 19

Step 3: Get Clear About Your Financial Means 27

Step 4: Track Your Credit Score 77

Step 5: Pay Down Your Debt 81

INTRODUCTION

Congratulations on taking the first step toward achieving your financial goals. Whether you want to pay off your credit cards, build up your savings account, increase your credit score, or make a large purchase, there's no better time to take control of your finances than now.

This book is broken down into 5 different sections:

Step 1: Determine My Money Mindset
Step 2: Set Financial Goals
Step 3: Set Your Monthly Budget
Step 4: Track Your Credit Score
Step 5: Pay Down Your Debt

In Step 1, you will start by identifying your financial mindset. By answering thought-provoking questions, you will gain insight into your personal relationship with money.

In Step 2, you will set short-term, mid-term, and long-term financial goals. Refer back to this section throughout the year to motivate yourself to reach the goals that you set. Writing down your financial goals is the first step toward bringing them to life.

In Step 3, you will find 12 months of budget planning pages you will use to develop a monthly spending plan. By creating a written budget and tracking your income, expenses, and spending, you will be much more likely to reach your financial goals . At the end of each month, you will reflect on your financial progress, celebrate your financial wins, and identify opportunities to cut down on your expenses and increase your income.

In Step 4, you will review and track your credit score.

In Step 5, you will use the debt tracking worksheets to track your debt.

$

STEP 1

Determine My Money Mindset

What Is My Unique Perspective On Money?

Try asking yourselves the following questions to help you uncover your unique perspective on money. In answering some of these questions, you may begin to develop a bigger, clearer picture of who you are with respect to your financial philosophy and money mindset. Being transparent about your thoughts and feelings will provide you with insight into your own triggers, fears, and expectation when it comes to your unique perspective on money.

Is money the root of all evil?

Do I shop to feel happy and complete?

Are expensive gifts a sign love?

What does money represent? Freedom? Power? Status? Security?

Am I generous with money to friends and family?

Do I abhor the wealthy?

Is financial discipline deprivation? Or, smart thinking?

Should my partner take care of me financially?

Is paying bills on time important?

Do I think about saving for the future? Or, spending in the present?

Do I hoard money for fear of being poor?

Do I spend excessively now because I was deprived as a child?

Do I lie about how much money I make to bolster my confidence?

Is talking about money impolite and a sign of poor home-training?

Do I worry about what others think about me so I always have to have the latest?

Did I grow up feeling poor?

How did my mother handle money?

How did my father handle money?

Was there enough money growing up?

If you had to classify yourself, would you identity as a "saver" or a "spender"?

What kind of lifestyle do you want to live? (jet-setting, minimalist, nomadic, suburban) and how much money will that cost?

What does "wealth" mean to you?

At what age do you want to retire?

STEP 2

Set Financial Goals

FINANCIAL GOALS

Whether you want to pay off your credit cards, build up your savings account, increase your credit score, or make a large purchase, writing down your financial goals is the first step toward bringing them to life. Use this section to list your financial goals and create an action plan to achieve each one.

FINANCIAL GOALS

Goal: ____

____

Challenges I May Encounter: ______________________________

____

Cost Estimate: ____________________ Target Date: ____________________

Steps to Take to Achieve This Goal: ______________________________

____

____

____

Why Is This Goal Important to Me? How will my life change once I achieve this goal?

____

____

____

Goal: ____

____

Challenges I May Encounter: ______________________________

____

Cost Estimate: ____________________ Target Date: ____________________

Steps to Take to Achieve This Goal: ______________________________

____

____

____

Why Is This Goal Important to Me? How will my life change once I achieve this goal?

____

____

____

FINANCIAL GOALS

Goal: ____

____

Challenges I May Encounter: ____

____

Cost Estimate: ____________________ Target Date: ____________________

Steps to Take to Achieve This Goal: ____

____

____

____

Why Is This Goal Important to Me? How will my life change once I achieve this goal?

____

____

____

Goal: ____

____

Challenges I May Encounter: ____

____

Cost Estimate: ____________________ Target Date: ____________________

Steps to Take to Achieve This Goal: ____

____

____

____

Why Is This Goal Important to Me? How will my life change once I achieve this goal?

____

____

____

FINANCIAL GOALS

Goal: ____

____

Challenges I May Encounter: ____

____

Cost Estimate: ____________________ Target Date: ____________________

Steps to Take to Achieve This Goal: ____

____

____

____

Why Is This Goal Important to Me? How will my life change once I achieve this goal?

____

____

____

Goal: ____

____

Challenges I May Encounter: ____

____

Cost Estimate: ____________________ Target Date: ____________________

Steps to Take to Achieve This Goal: ____

____

____

____

Why Is This Goal Important to Me? How will my life change once I achieve this goal?

____

____

____

FINANCIAL GOALS

Goal: ______________________________

____

Challenges I May Encounter: ______________________________

____

Cost Estimate: ______________ Target Date: ______________

Steps to Take to Achieve This Goal: ______________________________

____

____

____

Why Is This Goal Important to Me? How will my life change once I achieve this goal?

____

____

____

Goal: ______________________________

____

Challenges I May Encounter: ______________________________

____

Cost Estimate: ______________ Target Date: ______________

Steps to Take to Achieve This Goal: ______________________________

____

____

____

Why Is This Goal Important to Me? How will my life change once I achieve this goal?

____

____

____

FINANCIAL GOALS

Goal: ____
____

Challenges I May Encounter: ______________________________
____

Cost Estimate: ____________________ Target Date: ____________________

Steps to Take to Achieve This Goal: ______________________
____
____
____

Why Is This Goal Important to Me? How will my life change once I achieve this goal?
____
____
____

Goal: ____
____

Challenges I May Encounter: ______________________________
____

Cost Estimate: ____________________ Target Date: ____________________

Steps to Take to Achieve This Goal: ______________________
____
____
____

Why Is This Goal Important to Me? How will my life change once I achieve this goal?
____
____
____

$

STEP 3

Get Clear About Your Financial Means

MONTHLY BUDGET

MONTH OF:

Do you know where your money goes? In order to achieve your financial goals, you have to become a master of your money and there's no better way than by creating a monthly spending plan. Use this section to set a goal for the month, plan your monthly budget, and track your expenses and income. At the end of the month, review your progress.

THIS MONTH'S FINANCIAL GOALS

THIS MONTH'S TO DO ITEMS

- [ ]
- [ ]
- [ ]
- [ ]
- [ ]

UPCOMING PURCHASES/BILLS

HOUSING	BUDGET	ACTUAL
mortgage/rent	$	$
taxes	$	$
insurance	$	$
repairs	$	$
total	$	$

PERSONAL	BUDGET	ACTUAL
clothing	$	$
personal care	$	$
	$	$
	$	$
total	$	$

UTILITIES	BUDGET	ACTUAL
electricity	$	$
gas	$	$
trash	$	$
internet	$	$
phone	$	$
total	$	$

TRANSPORTATION	BUDGET	ACTUAL
car note	$	$
insurance	$	$
fuel	$	$
maintenance	$	$
taxi/rideshore/ train	$	$
total	$	$

FOOD	BUDGET	ACTUAL
groceries	$	$
eating out	$	$
total	$	$

HEALTH	BUDGET	ACTUAL
medical	$	$
insurance	$	$
total	$	$

DEBTS	BUDGET	ACTUAL
credit cards	$	$
loans	$	$
total	$	$

OTHER	BUDGET	ACTUAL
	$	$
	$	$
	$	$

INCOME		
date	source	amount
		$
		$
		$
total income	$	$

TOTAL INCOME ____________

\-

TOTAL EXPENSES ____________

=

DATE	ITEM	COST	WANT	NEED
			☐	☐
			☐	☐
			☐	☐
			☐	☐
			☐	☐
			☐	☐
			☐	☐
			☐	☐
			☐	☐
			☐	☐
			☐	☐
			☐	☐
			☐	☐
			☐	☐
			☐	☐
			☐	☐
			☐	☐
			☐	☐
			☐	☐
			☐	☐
			☐	☐
			☐	☐
			☐	☐
			☐	☐
			☐	☐
			☐	☐
			☐	☐
			☐	☐
			☐	☐
			☐	☐
			☐	☐
			☐	☐
			☐	☐
			☐	☐
			☐	☐

Congratulations! Now that you have reached the end of the month, it is time to complete your monthly review. Think of this as your financial progress report for the month. Did you spend less than you budgeted? Did you take steps to achieve a financial goal? Use this page to analyze your month and identify opportunities for improvement.

THIS MONTH'S FINANCIAL WINS

WHAT CAN I CHANGE OR IMPROVE?

NOTES

MONTHLY BUDGET

MONTH OF: ______________________

Do you know where your money goes? In order to achieve your financial goals, you have to become a master of your money and there's no better way than by creating a monthly spending plan. Use this section to set a goal for the month, plan your monthly budget, and track your expenses and income. At the end of the month, review your progress.

THIS MONTH'S FINANCIAL GOALS

____

____

____

____

____

THIS MONTH'S TO DO ITEMS

- ❑ ____
- ❑ ____
- ❑ ____
- ❑ ____
- ❑ ____

UPCOMING PURCHASES/BILLS	

HOUSING	BUDGET	ACTUAL
mortgage/rent	$	$
taxes	$	$
insurance	$	$
repairs	$	$
total	$	$

PERSONAL	BUDGET	ACTUAL
clothing	$	$
personal care	$	$
	$	$
	$	$
total	$	$

UTILITIES	BUDGET	ACTUAL
electricity	$	$
gas	$	$
trash	$	$
internet	$	$
phone	$	$
total	$	$

TRANSPORTATION	BUDGET	ACTUAL
car note	$	$
insurance	$	$
fuel	$	$
maintenance	$	$
taxi/rideshore/ train	$	$
total	$	$

FOOD	BUDGET	ACTUAL
groceries	$	$
eating out	$	$
total	$	$

HEALTH	BUDGET	ACTUAL
medical	$	$
insurance	$	$
total	$	$

DEBTS	BUDGET	ACTUAL
credit cards	$	$
loans	$	$
total	$	$

OTHER	BUDGET	ACTUAL
	$	$
	$	$
	$	$

INCOME		
date	source	amount
		$
		$
		$
total income	$	$

TOTAL INCOME

\-

TOTAL EXPENSES

=

DATE	ITEM	COST	WANT	NEED
			☐	☐
			☐	☐
			☐	☐
			☐	☐
			☐	☐
			☐	☐
			☐	☐
			☐	☐
			☐	☐
			☐	☐
			☐	☐
			☐	☐
			☐	☐
			☐	☐
			☐	☐
			☐	☐
			☐	☐
			☐	☐
			☐	☐
			☐	☐
			☐	☐
			☐	☐
			☐	☐
			☐	☐
			☐	☐
			☐	☐
			☐	☐
			☐	☐
			☐	☐
			☐	☐
			☐	☐
			☐	☐
			☐	☐
			☐	☐
			☐	☐

Congratulations! Now that you have reached the end of the month, it is time to complete your monthly review. Think of this as your financial progress report for the month. Did you spend less than you budgeted? Did you take steps to achieve a financial goal? Use this page to analyze your month and identify opportunities for improvement.

THIS MONTH'S FINANCIAL WINS

WHAT CAN I CHANGE OR IMPROVE?

NOTES

MONTHLY BUDGET

MONTH OF:

Do you know where your money goes? In order to achieve your financial goals, you have to become a master of your money and there's no better way than by creating a monthly spending plan. Use this section to set a goal for the month, plan your monthly budget, and track your expenses and income. At the end of the month, review your progress.

THIS MONTH'S FINANCIAL GOALS

THIS MONTH'S TO DO ITEMS

- ☐
- ☐
- ☐
- ☐
- ☐

UPCOMING PURCHASES/BILLS

HOUSING	BUDGET	ACTUAL
mortgage/rent	$	$
taxes	$	$
insurance	$	$
repairs	$	$
total	$	$

PERSONAL	BUDGET	ACTUAL
clothing	$	$
personal care	$	$
	$	$
	$	$
total	$	$

UTILITIES	BUDGET	ACTUAL
electricity	$	$
gas	$	$
trash	$	$
internet	$	$
phone	$	$
total	$	$

TRANSPORTATION	BUDGET	ACTUAL
car note	$	$
insurance	$	$
fuel	$	$
maintenance	$	$
taxi/rideshore/ train	$	$
total	$	$

FOOD	BUDGET	ACTUAL
groceries	$	$
eating out	$	$
total	$	$

HEALTH	BUDGET	ACTUAL
medical	$	$
insurance	$	$
total	$	$

DEBTS	BUDGET	ACTUAL
credit cards	$	$
loans	$	$
total	$	$

OTHER	BUDGET	ACTUAL
	$	$
	$	$
	$	$

INCOME		
date	source	amount
		$
		$
		$
total income	$	$

TOTAL INCOME ______

\-

TOTAL EXPENSES ______

=

DATE	ITEM	COST	WANT	NEED

Congratulations! Now that you have reached the end of the month, it is time to complete your monthly review. Think of this as your financial progress report for the month. Did you spend less than you budgeted? Did you take steps to achieve a financial goal? Use this page to analyze your month and identify opportunities for improvement.

THIS MONTH'S FINANCIAL WINS

WHAT CAN I CHANGE OR IMPROVE?

NOTES

MONTHLY BUDGET

MONTH OF:

Do you know where your money goes? In order to achieve your financial goals, you have to become a master of your money and there's no better way than by creating a monthly spending plan. Use this section to set a goal for the month, plan your monthly budget, and track your expenses and income. At the end of the month, review your progress.

THIS MONTH'S FINANCIAL GOALS

THIS MONTH'S TO DO ITEMS

- [ ]
- [ ]
- [ ]
- [ ]
- [ ]

UPCOMING PURCHASES/BILLS	

HOUSING	BUDGET	ACTUAL
mortgage/rent	$	$
taxes	$	$
insurance	$	$
repairs	$	$
total	$	$

PERSONAL	BUDGET	ACTUAL
clothing	$	$
personal care	$	$
	$	$
	$	$
total	$	$

UTILITIES	BUDGET	ACTUAL
electricity	$	$
gas	$	$
trash	$	$
internet	$	$
phone	$	$
total	$	$

TRANSPORTATION	BUDGET	ACTUAL
car note	$	$
insurance	$	$
fuel	$	$
maintenance	$	$
taxi/rideshore/ train	$	$
total	$	$

FOOD	BUDGET	ACTUAL
groceries	$	$
eating out	$	$
total	$	$

HEALTH	BUDGET	ACTUAL
medical	$	$
insurance	$	$
total	$	$

DEBTS	BUDGET	ACTUAL
credit cards	$	$
loans	$	$
total	$	$

OTHER	BUDGET	ACTUAL
	$	$
	$	$
	$	$

INCOME		
date	source	amount
		$
		$
		$
total income	$	$

TOTAL INCOME	
-	
TOTAL EXPENSES	
=	

DATE	ITEM	COST	WANT	NEED
			☐	☐
			☐	☐
			☐	☐
			☐	☐
			☐	☐
			☐	☐
			☐	☐
			☐	☐
			☐	☐
			☐	☐
			☐	☐
			☐	☐
			☐	☐
			☐	☐
			☐	☐
			☐	☐
			☐	☐
			☐	☐
			☐	☐
			☐	☐
			☐	☐
			☐	☐
			☐	☐
			☐	☐
			☐	☐
			☐	☐
			☐	☐
			☐	☐
			☐	☐
			☐	☐
			☐	☐
			☐	☐
			☐	☐
			☐	☐
			☐	☐

Congratulations! Now that you have reached the end of the month, it is time to complete your monthly review. Think of this as your financial progress report for the month. Did you spend less than you budgeted? Did you take steps to achieve a financial goal? Use this page to analyze your month and identify opportunities for improvement.

THIS MONTH'S FINANCIAL WINS

WHAT CAN I CHANGE OR IMPROVE?

NOTES

MONTHLY BUDGET

MONTH OF:

Do you know where your money goes? In order to achieve your financial goals, you have to become a master of your money and there's no better way than by creating a monthly spending plan. Use this section to set a goal for the month, plan your monthly budget, and track your expenses and income. At the end of the month, review your progress.

THIS MONTH'S FINANCIAL GOALS

THIS MONTH'S TO DO ITEMS

- [ ]
- [ ]
- [ ]
- [ ]
- [ ]

UPCOMING PURCHASES/BILLS

HOUSING	BUDGET	ACTUAL
mortgage/rent	$	$
taxes	$	$
insurance	$	$
repairs	$	$
total	$	$

PERSONAL	BUDGET	ACTUAL
clothing	$	$
personal care	$	$
	$	$
	$	$
total	$	$

UTILITIES	BUDGET	ACTUAL
electricity	$	$
gas	$	$
trash	$	$
internet	$	$
phone	$	$
total	$	$

TRANSPORTATION	BUDGET	ACTUAL
car note	$	$
insurance	$	$
fuel	$	$
maintenance	$	$
taxi/rideshore/ train	$	$
total	$	$

FOOD	BUDGET	ACTUAL
groceries	$	$
eating out	$	$
total	$	$

HEALTH	BUDGET	ACTUAL
medical	$	$
insurance	$	$
total	$	$

DEBTS	BUDGET	ACTUAL
credit cards	$	$
loans	$	$
total	$	$

OTHER	BUDGET	ACTUAL
	$	$
	$	$
	$	$

INCOME

date	source	amount
		$
		$
		$
total income	$	$

TOTAL INCOME	
-	
TOTAL EXPENSES	
=	

DATE	ITEM	COST	WANT	NEED
			☐	☐
			☐	☐
			☐	☐
			☐	☐
			☐	☐
			☐	☐
			☐	☐
			☐	☐
			☐	☐
			☐	☐
			☐	☐
			☐	☐
			☐	☐
			☐	☐
			☐	☐
			☐	☐
			☐	☐
			☐	☐
			☐	☐
			☐	☐
			☐	☐
			☐	☐
			☐	☐
			☐	☐
			☐	☐
			☐	☐
			☐	☐
			☐	☐
			☐	☐
			☐	☐
			☐	☐
			☐	☐
			☐	☐
			☐	☐
			☐	☐

Congratulations! Now that you have reached the end of the month, it is time to complete your monthly review. Think of this as your financial progress report for the month. Did you spend less than you budgeted? Did you take steps to achieve a financial goal? Use this page to analyze your month and identify opportunities for improvement.

THIS MONTH'S FINANCIAL WINS

WHAT CAN I CHANGE OR IMPROVE?

NOTES

MONTHLY BUDGET

MONTH OF:

Do you know where your money goes? In order to achieve your financial goals, you have to become a master of your money and there's no better way than by creating a monthly spending plan. Use this section to set a goal for the month, plan your monthly budget, and track your expenses and income. At the end of the month, review your progress.

THIS MONTH'S FINANCIAL GOALS

THIS MONTH'S TO DO ITEMS

- [ ]
- [ ]
- [ ]
- [ ]
- [ ]

UPCOMING PURCHASES/BILLS	

HOUSING	BUDGET	ACTUAL
mortgage/rent	$	$
taxes	$	$
insurance	$	$
repairs	$	$
total	$	$

PERSONAL	BUDGET	ACTUAL
clothing	$	$
personal care	$	$
	$	$
	$	$
total	$	$

UTILITIES	BUDGET	ACTUAL
electricity	$	$
gas	$	$
trash	$	$
internet	$	$
phone	$	$
total	$	$

TRANSPORTATION	BUDGET	ACTUAL
car note	$	$
insurance	$	$
fuel	$	$
maintenance	$	$
taxi/rideshore/ train	$	$
total	$	$

FOOD	BUDGET	ACTUAL
groceries	$	$
eating out	$	$
total	$	$

HEALTH	BUDGET	ACTUAL
medical	$	$
insurance	$	$
total	$	$

DEBTS	BUDGET	ACTUAL
credit cards	$	$
loans	$	$
total	$	$

OTHER	BUDGET	ACTUAL
	$	$
	$	$
	$	$

INCOME		
date	source	amount
		$
		$
		$
total income	$	$

TOTAL INCOME	
-	
TOTAL EXPENSES	
=	

DATE	ITEM	COST	WANT	NEED
			❑	❑
			❑	❑
			❑	❑
			❑	❑
			❑	❑
			❑	❑
			❑	❑
			❑	❑
			❑	❑
			❑	❑
			❑	❑
			❑	❑
			❑	❑
			❑	❑
			❑	❑
			❑	❑
			❑	❑
			❑	❑
			❑	❑
			❑	❑
			❑	❑
			❑	❑
			❑	❑
			❑	❑
			❑	❑
			❑	❑
			❑	❑
			❑	❑
			❑	❑
			❑	❑
			❑	❑
			❑	❑
			❑	❑
			❑	❑
			❑	❑

Congratulations! Now that you have reached the end of the month, it is time to complete your monthly review. Think of this as your financial progress report for the month. Did you spend less than you budgeted? Did you take steps to achieve a financial goal? Use this page to analyze your month and identify opportunities for improvement.

THIS MONTH'S FINANCIAL WINS

WHAT CAN I CHANGE OR IMPROVE?

NOTES

MONTHLY BUDGET

MONTH OF:

Do you know where your money goes? In order to achieve your financial goals, you have to become a master of your money and there's no better way than by creating a monthly spending plan. Use this section to set a goal for the month, plan your monthly budget, and track your expenses and income. At the end of the month, review your progress.

THIS MONTH'S FINANCIAL GOALS

THIS MONTH'S TO DO ITEMS

- [ ]
- [ ]
- [ ]
- [ ]
- [ ]

UPCOMING PURCHASES/BILLS

HOUSING	BUDGET	ACTUAL
mortgage/rent	$	$
taxes	$	$
insurance	$	$
repairs	$	$
total	$	$

PERSONAL	BUDGET	ACTUAL
clothing	$	$
personal care	$	$
	$	$
	$	$
total	$	$

UTILITIES	BUDGET	ACTUAL
electricity	$	$
gas	$	$
trash	$	$
internet	$	$
phone	$	$
total	$	$

TRANSPORTATION	BUDGET	ACTUAL
car note	$	$
insurance	$	$
fuel	$	$
maintenance	$	$
taxi/rideshore/ train	$	$
total	$	$

FOOD	BUDGET	ACTUAL
groceries	$	$
eating out	$	$
total	$	$

HEALTH	BUDGET	ACTUAL
medical	$	$
insurance	$	$
total	$	$

DEBTS	BUDGET	ACTUAL
credit cards	$	$
loans	$	$
total	$	$

OTHER	BUDGET	ACTUAL
	$	$
	$	$
	$	$

INCOME		
date	source	amount
		$
		$
		$
total income	$	$

TOTAL INCOME	
-	
TOTAL EXPENSES	
=	

DATE	ITEM	COST	WANT	NEED
			☐	☐
			☐	☐
			☐	☐
			☐	☐
			☐	☐
			☐	☐
			☐	☐
			☐	☐
			☐	☐
			☐	☐
			☐	☐
			☐	☐
			☐	☐
			☐	☐
			☐	☐
			☐	☐
			☐	☐
			☐	☐
			☐	☐
			☐	☐
			☐	☐
			☐	☐
			☐	☐
			☐	☐
			☐	☐
			☐	☐
			☐	☐
			☐	☐
			☐	☐
			☐	☐
			☐	☐
			☐	☐
			☐	☐
			☐	☐
			☐	☐

Congratulations! Now that you have reached the end of the month, it is time to complete your monthly review. Think of this as your financial progress report for the month. Did you spend less than you budgeted? Did you take steps to achieve a financial goal? Use this page to analyze your month and identify opportunities for improvement.

THIS MONTH'S FINANCIAL WINS

WHAT CAN I CHANGE OR IMPROVE?

NOTES

MONTHLY BUDGET

MONTH OF:

Do you know where your money goes? In order to achieve your financial goals, you have to become a master of your money and there's no better way than by creating a monthly spending plan. Use this section to set a goal for the month, plan your monthly budget, and track your expenses and income. At the end of the month, review your progress.

THIS MONTH'S FINANCIAL GOALS

THIS MONTH'S TO DO ITEMS

- [ ]
- [ ]
- [ ]
- [ ]
- [ ]

UPCOMING PURCHASES/BILLS

HOUSING	BUDGET	ACTUAL
mortgage/rent	$	$
taxes	$	$
insurance	$	$
repairs	$	$
total	$	$

PERSONAL	BUDGET	ACTUAL
clothing	$	$
personal care	$	$
	$	$
	$	$
total	$	$

UTILITIES	BUDGET	ACTUAL
electricity	$	$
gas	$	$
trash	$	$
internet	$	$
phone	$	$
total	$	$

TRANSPORTATION	BUDGET	ACTUAL
car note	$	$
insurance	$	$
fuel	$	$
maintenance	$	$
taxi/rideshore/ train	$	$
total	$	$

FOOD	BUDGET	ACTUAL
groceries	$	$
eating out	$	$
total	$	$

HEALTH	BUDGET	ACTUAL
medical	$	$
insurance	$	$
total	$	$

DEBTS	BUDGET	ACTUAL
credit cards	$	$
loans	$	$
total	$	$

OTHER	BUDGET	ACTUAL
	$	$
	$	$
	$	$

INCOME		
date	source	amount
		$
		$
		$
total income	$	$

TOTAL INCOME	
-	
TOTAL EXPENSES	
=	

DATE	ITEM	COST	WANT	NEED
			☐	☐
			☐	☐
			☐	☐
			☐	☐
			☐	☐
			☐	☐
			☐	☐
			☐	☐
			☐	☐
			☐	☐
			☐	☐
			☐	☐
			☐	☐
			☐	☐
			☐	☐
			☐	☐
			☐	☐
			☐	☐
			☐	☐
			☐	☐
			☐	☐
			☐	☐
			☐	☐
			☐	☐
			☐	☐
			☐	☐
			☐	☐
			☐	☐
			☐	☐
			☐	☐
			☐	☐
			☐	☐
			☐	☐
			☐	☐
			☐	☐

Congratulations! Now that you have reached the end of the month, it is time to complete your monthly review. Think of this as your financial progress report for the month. Did you spend less than you budgeted? Did you take steps to achieve a financial goal? Use this page to analyze your month and identify opportunities for improvement.

THIS MONTH'S FINANCIAL WINS

WHAT CAN I CHANGE OR IMPROVE?

NOTES

MONTHLY BUDGET

MONTH OF:

Do you know where your money goes? In order to achieve your financial goals, you have to become a master of your money and there's no better way than by creating a monthly spending plan. Use this section to set a goal for the month, plan your monthly budget, and track your expenses and income. At the end of the month, review your progress.

THIS MONTH'S FINANCIAL GOALS

THIS MONTH'S TO DO ITEMS

- [ ]
- [ ]
- [ ]
- [ ]
- [ ]

UPCOMING PURCHASES/BILLS

HOUSING	BUDGET	ACTUAL
mortgage/rent	$	$
taxes	$	$
insurance	$	$
repairs	$	$
total	$	$

PERSONAL	BUDGET	ACTUAL
clothing	$	$
personal care	$	$
	$	$
	$	$
total	$	$

UTILITIES	BUDGET	ACTUAL
electricity	$	$
gas	$	$
trash	$	$
internet	$	$
phone	$	$
total	$	$

TRANSPORTATION	BUDGET	ACTUAL
car note	$	$
insurance	$	$
fuel	$	$
maintenance	$	$
taxi/rideshore/ train	$	$
total	$	$

FOOD	BUDGET	ACTUAL
groceries	$	$
eating out	$	$
total	$	$

HEALTH	BUDGET	ACTUAL
medical	$	$
insurance	$	$
total	$	$

DEBTS	BUDGET	ACTUAL
credit cards	$	$
loans	$	$
total	$	$

OTHER	BUDGET	ACTUAL
	$	$
	$	$
	$	$

INCOME		
date	source	amount
		$
		$
		$
total income	$	$

TOTAL INCOME

-

TOTAL EXPENSES

=

DATE	ITEM	COST	WANT	NEED
			❑	❑
			❑	❑
			❑	❑
			❑	❑
			❑	❑
			❑	❑
			❑	❑
			❑	❑
			❑	❑
			❑	❑
			❑	❑
			❑	❑
			❑	❑
			❑	❑
			❑	❑
			❑	❑
			❑	❑
			❑	❑
			❑	❑
			❑	❑
			❑	❑
			❑	❑
			❑	❑
			❑	❑
			❑	❑
			❑	❑
			❑	❑
			❑	❑
			❑	❑
			❑	❑
			❑	❑
			❑	❑
			❑	❑
			❑	❑
			❑	❑

Congratulations! Now that you have reached the end of the month, it is time to complete your monthly review. Think of this as your financial progress report for the month. Did you spend less than you budgeted? Did you take steps to achieve a financial goal? Use this page to analyze your month and identify opportunities for improvement.

THIS MONTH'S FINANCIAL WINS

WHAT CAN I CHANGE OR IMPROVE?

NOTES

MONTHLY BUDGET

MONTH OF:

Do you know where your money goes? In order to achieve your financial goals, you have to become a master of your money and there's no better way than by creating a monthly spending plan. Use this section to set a goal for the month, plan your monthly budget, and track your expenses and income. At the end of the month, review your progress.

THIS MONTH'S FINANCIAL GOALS

THIS MONTH'S TO DO ITEMS

- [ ]
- [ ]
- [ ]
- [ ]
- [ ]

UPCOMING PURCHASES/BILLS

HOUSING	BUDGET	ACTUAL
mortgage/rent	$	$
taxes	$	$
insurance	$	$
repairs	$	$
total	$	$

PERSONAL	BUDGET	ACTUAL
clothing	$	$
personal care	$	$
	$	$
	$	$
total	$	$

UTILITIES	BUDGET	ACTUAL
electricity	$	$
gas	$	$
trash	$	$
internet	$	$
phone	$	$
total	$	$

TRANSPORTATION	BUDGET	ACTUAL
car note	$	$
insurance	$	$
fuel	$	$
maintenance	$	$
taxi/rideshore/ train	$	$
total	$	$

FOOD	BUDGET	ACTUAL
groceries	$	$
eating out	$	$
total	$	$

HEALTH	BUDGET	ACTUAL
medical	$	$
insurance	$	$
total	$	$

DEBTS	BUDGET	ACTUAL
credit cards	$	$
loans	$	$
total	$	$

OTHER	BUDGET	ACTUAL
	$	$
	$	$
	$	$

INCOME		
date	source	amount
		$
		$
		$
total income	$	$

TOTAL INCOME	
-	
TOTAL EXPENSES	
=	

DATE	ITEM	COST	WANT	NEED
			☐	☐
			☐	☐
			☐	☐
			☐	☐
			☐	☐
			☐	☐
			☐	☐
			☐	☐
			☐	☐
			☐	☐
			☐	☐
			☐	☐
			☐	☐
			☐	☐
			☐	☐
			☐	☐
			☐	☐
			☐	☐
			☐	☐
			☐	☐
			☐	☐
			☐	☐
			☐	☐
			☐	☐
			☐	☐
			☐	☐
			☐	☐
			☐	☐
			☐	☐
			☐	☐
			☐	☐
			☐	☐
			☐	☐
			☐	☐
			☐	☐

Congratulations! Now that you have reached the end of the month, it is time to complete your monthly review. Think of this as your financial progress report for the month. Did you spend less than you budgeted? Did you take steps to achieve a financial goal? Use this page to analyze your month and identify opportunities for improvement.

THIS MONTH'S FINANCIAL WINS

WHAT CAN I CHANGE OR IMPROVE?

NOTES

MONTHLY BUDGET

MONTH OF:

Do you know where your money goes? In order to achieve your financial goals, you have to become a master of your money and there's no better way than by creating a monthly spending plan. Use this section to set a goal for the month, plan your monthly budget, and track your expenses and income. At the end of the month, review your progress.

THIS MONTH'S FINANCIAL GOALS

THIS MONTH'S TO DO ITEMS

- [ ]
- [ ]
- [ ]
- [ ]
- [ ]

UPCOMING PURCHASES/BILLS

HOUSING	BUDGET	ACTUAL
mortgage/rent	$	$
taxes	$	$
insurance	$	$
repairs	$	$
total	$	$

PERSONAL	BUDGET	ACTUAL
clothing	$	$
personal care	$	$
	$	$
	$	$
total	$	$

UTILITIES	BUDGET	ACTUAL
electricity	$	$
gas	$	$
trash	$	$
internet	$	$
phone	$	$
total	$	$

TRANSPORTATION	BUDGET	ACTUAL
car note	$	$
insurance	$	$
fuel	$	$
maintenance	$	$
taxi/rideshore/ train	$	$
total	$	$

FOOD	BUDGET	ACTUAL
groceries	$	$
eating out	$	$
total	$	$

HEALTH	BUDGET	ACTUAL
medical	$	$
insurance	$	$
total	$	$

DEBTS	BUDGET	ACTUAL
credit cards	$	$
loans	$	$
total	$	$

OTHER	BUDGET	ACTUAL
	$	$
	$	$
	$	$

INCOME		
date	source	amount
		$
		$
		$
total income	$	$

TOTAL INCOME

\-

TOTAL EXPENSES

=

DATE	ITEM	COST	WANT	NEED
			☐	☐
			☐	☐
			☐	☐
			☐	☐
			☐	☐
			☐	☐
			☐	☐
			☐	☐
			☐	☐
			☐	☐
			☐	☐
			☐	☐
			☐	☐
			☐	☐
			☐	☐
			☐	☐
			☐	☐
			☐	☐
			☐	☐
			☐	☐
			☐	☐
			☐	☐
			☐	☐
			☐	☐
			☐	☐
			☐	☐
			☐	☐
			☐	☐
			☐	☐
			☐	☐
			☐	☐
			☐	☐
			☐	☐
			☐	☐
			☐	☐

Congratulations! Now that you have reached the end of the month, it is time to complete your monthly review. Think of this as your financial progress report for the month. Did you spend less than you budgeted? Did you take steps to achieve a financial goal? Use this page to analyze your month and identify opportunities for improvement.

THIS MONTH'S FINANCIAL WINS

WHAT CAN I CHANGE OR IMPROVE?

NOTES

$

STEP 4

Track Your Credit Score

Your credit score is a three digit number that is calculated based on your credit history. It is important to take control of your credit score because it determines your eligibility for credit cards, home and auto loans, student loans, apartment rentals, and even some jobs.

The FICO scale ranges from 300 and 850 and your rating is rated according to the following scale:

Credit Score Rating

760 - 849 Excellent
700 - 759 Great
660 - 699 Good
620 - 659 Fair
580 - 619 Poor
579 - below Very Poor

Make a habit of reviewing your credit reports for errors and keeping track of your credit score.

Use this section to stay on top of your credit score by tracking it every month.

CREDIT SCORE TRACKER

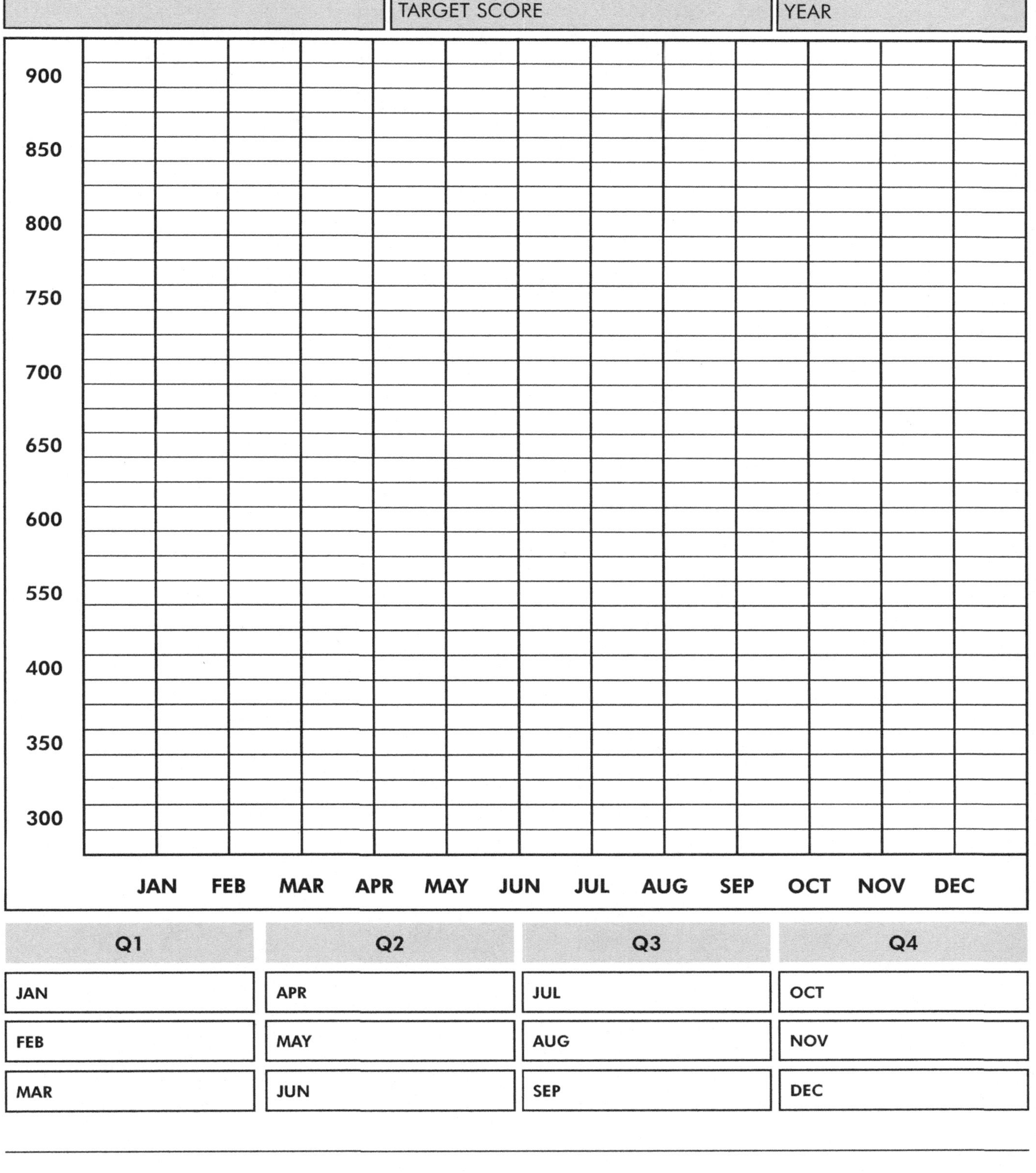

STEP 5

Pay Down Your Debt

DEBT TRACKER

DEBT NAME	STARTING BALANCE	MINIMUM PAYMENT

DATE	AMOUNT PAID	BALANCE

DEBT NAME	STARTING BALANCE	MINIMUM PAYMENT

DATE	AMOUNT PAID	BALANCE

DEBT TRACKER

DEBT NAME	STARTING BALANCE	MINIMUM PAYMENT

DATE	AMOUNT PAID	BALANCE

DEBT NAME	STARTING BALANCE	MINIMUM PAYMENT

DATE	AMOUNT PAID	BALANCE

DEBT TRACKER

DEBT NAME	STARTING BALANCE	MINIMUM PAYMENT

DATE	AMOUNT PAID	BALANCE

DEBT NAME	STARTING BALANCE	MINIMUM PAYMENT

DATE	AMOUNT PAID	BALANCE

DEBT TRACKER

DEBT NAME	STARTING BALANCE	MINIMUM PAYMENT

DATE	AMOUNT PAID	BALANCE

DEBT NAME	STARTING BALANCE	MINIMUM PAYMENT

DATE	AMOUNT PAID	BALANCE

DEBT TRACKER

DEBT NAME	STARTING BALANCE	MINIMUM PAYMENT

DATE	AMOUNT PAID	BALANCE

DEBT NAME	STARTING BALANCE	MINIMUM PAYMENT

DATE	AMOUNT PAID	BALANCE

DEBT TRACKER

DEBT NAME	STARTING BALANCE	MINIMUM PAYMENT

DATE	AMOUNT PAID	BALANCE

DEBT NAME	STARTING BALANCE	MINIMUM PAYMENT

DATE	AMOUNT PAID	BALANCE

Made in the USA
Columbia, SC
03 December 2024